First World War
and Army of Occupation
War Diary
France, Belgium and Germany

63 (ROYAL NAVAL) DIVISION
188 Infantry Brigade,
Brigade Trench Mortar Battery
1 July 1916 - 31 July 1916

WO95/3111/5

The Naval & Military Press Ltd
www.nmarchive.com
Published in association with The National Archives

Published by

The Naval & Military Press Ltd

Unit 10 Ridgewood Industrial Park,

Uckfield, East Sussex,

TN22 5QE England

Tel: +44 (0) 1825 749494

www.naval-military-press.com

www.nmarchive.com

This diary has been reprinted in facsimile from the original. Any imperfections are inevitably reproduced and the quality may fall short of modern type and cartographic standards.

© Crown Copyright
Images reproduced by permission of The National Archives, London, England, 2015.

Contents

Document type	Place/Title	Date From	Date To
Heading	WO95/3111-5		
Heading	63rd Division 188th Infy Bde 188th Lt. Trench Mortar Bty Jly 1916		
Heading	War Diary of 188th Light Trench Mortar Battery 63rd (RN) Division For Month Ending July 31st 1916		
War Diary	Hermin	01/07/1916	08/07/1916
War Diary	Villers-Au-Bois	09/07/1916	09/07/1916
War Diary	In The Trenches	10/07/1916	11/07/1916
War Diary	Villers-Au-Bois	12/07/1916	16/07/1916
War Diary	Hersin	15/07/1916	18/07/1916
War Diary	Bully-Grenay	19/07/1916	19/07/1916
War Diary	In The Trenches	20/07/1916	31/07/1916

WO95/31110 (5)

WO95/31110 (5)

63RD DIVISION
188TH INFY BDE

188TH LT. TRENCH MORTAR BTY

JLY 1916.

CONFIDENTIAL 63 | July
Vol I
188. T.M.B

War Diary
of
188th LIGHT TRENCH MORTAR
BATTERY.
63rd (RN) Division

For month ending July 31st 1916.

Alan Campbell Lieut RNVR.
Cmdg. 188th L.T.M. Battery
63rd (RN) Division

Army Form C. 2118.

WAR DIARY
or
INTELLIGENCE SUMMARY
(Erase heading not required.)

Instructions regarding War Diaries and Intelligence Summaries are contained in F. S. Regs., Part II. and the Staff Manual respectively. Title pages will be prepared in manuscript.

Place	Date	Hour	Summary of Events and Information	Remarks and references to Appendices
Hermin	1st July 1916		Firing carried out with dummy shells – gun fire and action fire practised.	R.D
Hermin	2nd July		Inspection by O.C Battery. Church Parade	R.D
Hermin	3rd July		Rocking Parade – marched to Bocks at Incourcourt. Inspection of arms, gas helmets and goggles. Practised firing	R.D
Hermin	4th July		Ammunition reissue inspected and emplacement positions concealed. Lecture by O.C Battery – "Use of French Mortars in Open Warfare"	R.D
			2/Lieut M.B. Walker promoted to Acting Captain and returned to 1st R.M. Battalion	R.D
Hermin	5th July		N.C.O.s and men (5 from 1st R.M Battalion, 5 from 2nd R.M Battalion, 10 from "Howe" Battalion) attached for instruction.	
			Lectures on use and parts of Guns; setting, firing and cleaning Guns; causes of and remedies for miss-fires; etc	R.D
Hermin	6th July		Gun-drill for men under instruction. Battery finished and elaborated ammunition recesses. Practice firing with Red and Green Cartridges.	R.D
Hermin	7th July		Instructed to stand by for orders to move forward. Men under instruction returned to units. Issue of clothing.	R.D
Hermin	8th July		Battery marched from Hermin to Villers-au-bois and was attached to 5th Brigade 2nd Division. Sub-Lieut Oakes (of "Anson Batt") joined up with Battery temporarily (vice Adj. Capt Walker)	R.D
Villers-au-bois	9th July		Standing by to proceed to trenches. Inspection Parade	R.D
In the Trenches	10th July		O.C Battery proceeded to Sector during forenoon and after alternative emplacements. Battery reached Sector after dusk and carried on digging emplacements. With handicapped by heavy rain, by numerous lights and projectile and by German Machine-gun fire	R.D
In the Trenches	11th July		Battery returned to Villers-au-bois at dawn, proceeding again to trenches in the evening. Alternative emplacements and communicating trenches were deepened, good progress being made as satisfactory cover had been obtained by previous nights digging. Work continued until dawn.	R.D

T.J.134. Wt. W708—776. 500000. 4/15. Sir J. C. & S.

Army Form C. 2118.

WAR DIARY
or
INTELLIGENCE SUMMARY.
(Erase heading not required.)

Instructions regarding War Diaries and Intelligence Summaries are contained in F. S. Regs., Part II. and the Staff Manual respectively. Title pages will be prepared in manuscript.

Place	Date	Hour	Summary of Events and Information	Remarks and references to Appendices
Villers-au-bois	12th July 1916		Returned from trenches at dawn. Received instructions that emplacement-digging was to be temporarily suspended.	R.O.
Villers-au-bois	13th July		Inspection Parade. Cleaned guns and haversacks.	R.O.
Villers-au-bois	14th July		Kit Inspection. Gas helmet drill and Gun-drill while wearing gas-helmets.	R.D.
Villers-au-bois	15th July		Cleaned guns. Ammunition removed from dumps, cleaned and prepared.	R.D.
Haram	16th July		Battery marched from Villers-au-bois to Haram, and was attached to the 47th Division.	R.D.
Haram	17th July		Standing by to receive orders. Inspection Parade.	R.O.
Haram	18th July		Inspection Parade. Gas Helmet Drill.	R.D.
Bully Grenay	19th July		Battery marched from Haram to Bully-Grenay and bivouaced. Officers and N.C.O.s visited sector to be taken over.	R.D.
In the Trenches	20th July		R.N.V.R. Section took over Guns and Advanced Headquarters of 3rd Brigade Light Trench Mortar Battery. Guns cleaned and prepared. Guns and ammunition. R.M.L.I. Section remained in billets at Bully.	
			26 mm (from 1st Marine, 2nd Marine, Anson and Hood Batt'ns) were attached to Battery this date.	R.D.
In the Trenches	21st July		Battery becomes 188th Light Trench Mortar Battery, attached to 63rd (Royal Naval) Division. Battery retaliated to German Mortars during afternoon. Permission was obtained to construct new gunpits and that work when commenced.	R.D
In the Trenches	22nd July		Battery fired during afternoon in conjunction with Heavy and Medium Mortars. Enemy made only very slight retaliation but shelled the communication trenches heavily in the evening. Work on gunpits was delayed by this bombardment. Progress only being made where good cover could be obtained.	R.D.

T2134. Wt. W708—776. 500000. 4/15. Sir J. C. & S.

Army Form C. 2118.

Instructions regarding War Diaries and Intelligence Summaries are contained in F.S. Regs., Part II. and the Staff Manual respectively. Title pages will be prepared in manuscript.

WAR DIARY
or
INTELLIGENCE SUMMARY.
(Erase heading not required.)

Place	Date	Hour	Summary of Events and Information	Remarks and references to Appendices
In the Trenches	23rd July 1916		R.M.L.I. Section was relieved by R.M.L.I. Section and returned to billets in Bully. Situation was very quiet.	
In the Trenches	24th July		Gun-pits work continued by working party. L.S. O'Hara went to F.A. suffering from a slight scalp wound and shock, received yesterday from burst of 2" mortar. R.D.	
			Two working parties of 20 workers on gunpits during day and one party of 50 worked during night. Considerable progress being made.	
			Afternoon party was prevented from working by enemy mortars to which Battery replied. R.D.	
In the Trenches	25th July		No working parties being available to-day. Apart men from crew continued work on gunpits.	
			Enemy artillery and mortars were very active, and Battery assisted in retaliation. R.D.	
In the Trenches	26th July		Working-parties continued on gunpits. Minenwerfer dropped shells near No. 6 Gun, apparently searching for it. R.D.	
In the Trenches	27th July		R.M.L.I. Section were relieved by R.N.V.R. Section. Working parties continued on gun-pits. R.D.	
In the Trenches	28th July		Battery co-operated with Artillery and Heavy Mortars about midnight. Enemy retaliated only feebly. Working-parties carried on with no gun-pits and commencing traverse. R.D.	
In the Trenches	29th July		Working-parties continued gun-pits. Battery fired in retaliation but situation was fairly quiet. R.D.	
In the Trenches	30th July		Enemy was very active with rifle grenades and mortars, and Battery retaliated by firing 45 rounds. Working parties continued gun-pits but work was frequently interrupted by enemy activity. R.D.	
In the Trenches	31st July		Enemy activity continued with rifle grenades and trench-mortars. Battery fired 70 rounds in retaliation. Working-parties carried on with gun-pits. R.D.	

www.ingramcontent.com/pod-product-compliance
Lightning Source LLC
Chambersburg PA
CBHW081517160426
43193CB00014B/2717